Native American

ART & CULTURE

Brendan January

www.raintreepublishers.co.uk
Visit our website to find out more information about **Raintree** books.

To order:
☎ Phone 44 (0)1865 888113
▤ Send a fax to 44 (0)1865 314091
▢ Visit the Raintree bookshop at **www.raintreepublishers.co.uk** to browse our catalogue and order online.

Produced for Raintree by
White-Thomson Publishing Ltd
Bridgewater Business Centre, 210 High Street,
Lewes, East Sussex BN7 2NH.

First published in Great Britain by Raintree,
Halley Court, Jordan Hill, Oxford OX2 8EJ,
part of Harcourt Education.
Raintree is a registered trademark of Harcourt Education Ltd.

© Harcourt Education Ltd 2005
The moral right of the proprietor has been asserted.

Editorial: Kay Barnham, Nicole Irving, Louise Galpine, and Carrie Radabaugh
Design: Simon Borrough and Ron Kamen
Illustrations: Tinstar Design
Picture research: Elaine Fuoco-Lang
Production: Amanda Meaden

Originated by Ambassador Litho Ltd
Printed and bound in Hong Kong, China, by South China Printing Company

ISBN 1 844 21056 1
09 08 07 06 05
10 9 8 7 6 5 4 3 2 1

British Library Cataloguing in Publication Data
January, Brendan
    World Art and Culture: Native American
    704'.0397
A full catalogue record for this book is available from the British Library.

Acknowledgements
The publishers would like to thank the following for permission to reproduce photographs:
Art Archive/National Archives p. **24**; Corbis pp. **6**, **9**, **11** (Gerrit Greve/Corbis), **15**, **16**, **20**, **21**, **26** (Ainaco/Corbis), **27** (Ainaco/Corbis), **29** (Kevin R. Morris/Corbis), **33**, **34**, **35**, **37**, **39**, **48**, **49**, **50** (Vince Steano/Corbis), **51**; Dennis MacDonald / Photo Edit p. **40**; Getty Images/Photodisc pp. **14**, **19**; Peter Newark's American Pictures pp. **10**, **44**; Topfoto p. **17**; Werner Forman Archive pp. **5**, **7**, **12**, **13**, **18**, **25**, **30**, **31**, **32**, **35**, **36**, **38**, **41**, **42**, **43**, **45**, **46**, **47**.

Cover photograph of mask reproduced with kind permission of Corbis/Seattle Art Museum, and of background cloth, reproduced with kind permission of Bridgeman Art Library.

The publishers would like to thank Traci Maday for her assistance in the preparation of this book.

Every effort has been made to contact copyright holders of any material reproduced in this book. Any omissions will be rectified in subsequent printings if notice is given to the publishers.

The paper used to print this book comes from sustainable resources.

Contents

Words printed in the text in bold, **like this**, are explained in the Glossary.

Introduction

The vast continent of North America stretches thousands of kilometres, from icy Arctic regions in the north to sun-baked landscapes in the south. It is bordered by two enormous oceans – the Atlantic and the Pacific.

Different landscapes

Many types of landscape can be found here. The east is marked by thick forests, while the Great Plains are grassy flatlands that extend across the middle of North America. In the west, the jagged, snow-capped Rocky Mountains rise up, and the southwest is mostly **arid**. Dense, moist pine forests carpet the northwest coast, beside the Pacific Ocean. The northern fringes of the continent are locked in snow and ice for most of the year.

Different peoples, different art

Thousands of years ago, most likely between 18,000 and 15,000 BCE, historians believe that people began arriving in North America from Asia. Native American **creation stories**, however, teach that each group of people was created on the land where they originally lived. Regardless of how they arrived, the first people **adapted** to the various landscapes and developed distinct cultural **traits**.

Art forms and lifestyles changed with exposure to different environments. In the southwest, the people became farmers. They built elaborate **irrigation** systems to keep their crops watered in the dry climate, lived in villages of mud brick, and created sand paintings.

Over a period of thousands of years, Native Americans populated all corners of North America. This vast land mass, with its enormous variety of climates and landscapes, influenced the development of astonishingly different cultures. The numbers on this map represent the general area each tribe inhabited around the time of European arrival to North America, as well as the locations of some of the ancient Native American groups.

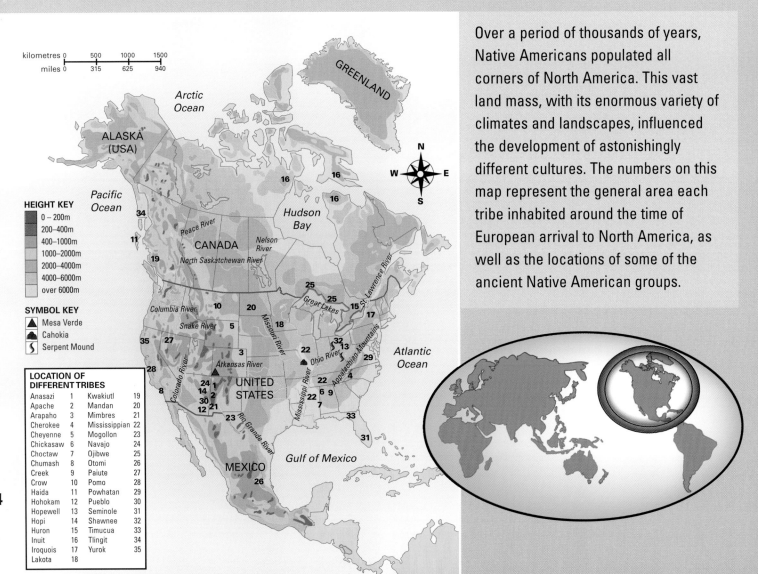

kilometres 0   500   1000   1500
miles 0   315   625   940

HEIGHT KEY
- 0 – 200m
- 200–400m
- 400–1000m
- 1000–2000m
- 2000–4000m
- 4000–6000m
- over 6000m

SYMBOL KEY
- ▲ Mesa Verde
- ⬟ Cahokia
- ⌇ Serpent Mound

LOCATION OF DIFFERENT TRIBES

Anasazi	1	Kwakiutl	19
Apache	2	Mandan	20
Arapaho	3	Mimbres	21
Cherokee	4	Mississippian	22
Cheyenne	5	Mogollon	23
Chickasaw	6	Navajo	24
Choctaw	7	Ojibwe	25
Chumash	8	Otomi	26
Creek	9	Paiute	27
Crow	10	Pomo	28
Haida	11	Powhatan	29
Hohokam	12	Pueblo	30
Hopewell	13	Seminole	31
Hopi	14	Shawnee	32
Huron	15	Timucua	33
Inuit	16	Tlingit	34
Iroquois	17	Yurok	35
Lakota	18		

4

In the northwest, people harvested food from the Pacific Ocean, which teemed with crabs, whales, and salmon. The surrounding forests provided wood for carvings, **totem poles**, masks, and lodges.

On the Great Plains, people hunted vast herds of buffalo. Every part of the animal was used – its meat for food, its skin for **teepees** and beaded clothing, and its bones for tools.

A number of cultures flourished and then faded in the eastern woodlands. They left behind stone carvings and giant earth mound structures along the banks of the Mississippi and Ohio Rivers, two wide waterways that drain through the continent. The size and complexity of these structures still amaze observers today.

In the frozen northern areas, the Inuit people made a life based on hunting. They created structures built from large blocks of ice.

Unique art

In each region of North America, **indigenous** peoples designed and developed unique art forms based on the availability of local materials, tools, and technologies. Trade routes enabled the exchange of foods, ideas, and materials between tribes, but art was most often distinct and sacred to each individual group.

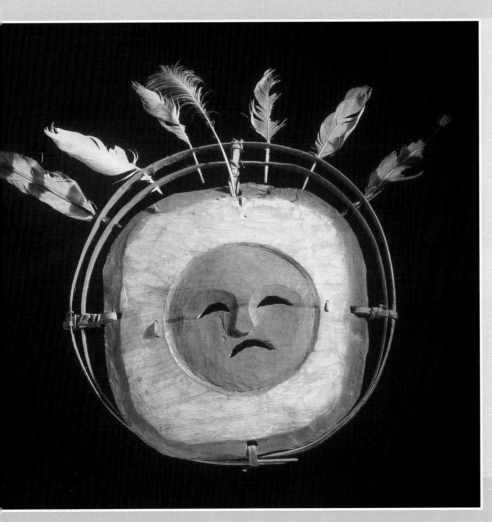

For Native Americans, art is not meant to be placed in a museum and viewed from afar. Rather, it is seen as an outward, physical expression of one's inner spirit. The symbols used in the art have meanings that go beneath the surface. For example, this mask – made by an artist in the region known today as Alaska – was filled with spirit and purpose. The face represents the moon, the space around the face is the night air, and the feathers above are the stars.

Arrival in North America

People disagree on the date of the first Native Americans' arrival in North America. Traditional Native American stories say that the tribes have been there since the time of creation. Some historians argue that people arrived 30,000 years ago, while others think that it may have been as early as 60,000 years ago. Most historians believe that a large **migration** took place between 18,000 and 15,000 BCE. At that time, an **Ice Age** froze billions of litres of water, causing ocean levels to fall and uncovering a land bridge between Alaska and Asia. Indigenous tribes probably crossed over this strip of land and spread south and east, following large **game** such as elk and mammoths.

These people gradually formed tribes – groups that shared a culture and language. Some tribes

The first Native Americans took shelter in caves, such as this cave in Utah, where they often left behind rock paintings.

continued to move, settling in some places for a time and then moving on. Meanwhile, others remained in the same area for centuries.

A second wave of migration occurred around 8000 BCE. By this time, the Ice Age had ended and the land bridge was once more covered by water. These new settlers probably came to North America in boats and canoes. Between the two large migrations, smaller groups also made their way to North America. So many tribes lived in so many areas that an historical overview can help us place each group and its art in context.

18,000–15,000 BCE: a land bridge between Alaska and Asia enables mass migration; arrowheads were used in hunting

8000 BCE: a second wave of mass migration to North America takes place; rock art documents what indigenous peoples found important

200 BCE –1000 CE: the Hopewell build vast mound complexes in the eastern woodlands and leave behind **artefacts** carved from stone

Pre-European North America

Native American cultures flourished in North America before the arrival of Europeans. Their ways of life, their beliefs, and their art were all closely tied to their physical surroundings.

In the arid southwest, early Native Americans lived **nomadic** lives, sheltering mostly in caves. They hunted fresh game and gathered roots and berries. Some of these people gradually established small farms and gathered together in villages, which eventually evolved into complex civilizations. Among the first recognizable cultures in the American southwest were the Mogollon, the Hohokam, and the Anasazi (450 BCE–1400 CE).

These cultures dug irrigation ditches to water their fields of corn. This reliable food source of farmed crops largely freed the people from the uncertain and time-consuming process of finding food. Stable and prosperous, they created a tradition of great craftsmanship. Today, their descendants are known for their baskets, weaving, and painted pottery.

Native Americans also spread into the forested regions between the Atlantic Ocean and the Mississippi River. The Hopewell culture was centred in present-day Ohio between about 200 BCE and 1000 CE. These people built elaborate mounds of earth. The mounds were used as tombs or as sites for important ceremonies. These mounds were sacred, and the Hopewell people buried a number of artistic objects there. They were expert carvers who produced remarkable stone sculptures and works from copper.

Native Americans set up complex trade routes and were therefore able to share parts of their culture. For example, seashells from Florida, **mica** from the Appalachian Mountains, and copper from the Great Lakes have all been found in the Hopewell mounds of southern Ohio.

The earliest examples of Native American tools are spearheads and arrowheads, like this arrowhead made between 300 BCE and 500 CE.

450 BCE–1400 CE: the Mogollon, Anasazi, and Hohokam people, known for their boldly patterned pottery, thrive in the southwest

900–1700 CE: Mississippian cultures grow and flourish in the Mississippi River valley, leaving behind massive earthen structures

1492: Christopher Columbus lands on islands in the West Indies, paving the way for European settlers who will change North America forever

The exploration of North America

In October 1492, three European ships appeared near the West Indies, in the Caribbean. The commander of the ships, an Italian named Christopher Columbus who worked for the Spanish, was looking for a trade route to India. When he spied islands off the coast of North America, he mistakenly believed he had reached India and called the first people he saw 'Indians'.

In reality, Columbus had reached the outskirts of a vast continent occupied by hundreds of diverse cultures. Modern estimates of the Native American population in 1492 vary, but it is generally accepted that there were at least two million people, speaking 400 or more different languages. Some estimates place the number at almost 30 million people.

It is likely that several explorers had reached North America before Columbus, but it is certain that many more explorers came after him. In 1513, a Spanish explorer named Juan Ponce de León entered the swamps of Florida. In 1541, fellow countryman Francisco Vázquez de Coronado crossed the deserts of the southwest. Meanwhile, the French and English explored the northeast and mapped the area where the giant St Lawrence River flows into the Great Lakes.

The Europeans did not just explore North America. They also settled there, building towns with homes and churches, and often displacing Native Americans as they went. In 1565, the Spanish built the first permanent European **colony** on the North American mainland at St Augustine, Florida. In 1607, a group of English settlers landed on the east coast and established a settlement called Jamestown, Virginia. In 1608, the French established a colony in Quebec, Canada. In 1620, a group of English **Puritans**, seeking religious freedom, sailed from Plymouth, England, and settled in Massachusetts. Slowly but relentlessly, Europeans began building the settlements that would drastically alter North America.

Interactions

In the east, Native Americans and settlers were often friendly at first. Settlers learned how to farm and hunt the plants and animals of their new environment with Native American help. In Canada, local tribes began a brisk trade with the French. The French exchanged metal pots and axes, glass beads, and guns for the fur **pelts** offered by Native Americans.

These friendly feelings did not last. Europeans wanted to create vast farms, but Native Americans, while they believed that it was acceptable for individual groups to live and hunt on a particular area of land, did not consider that the land was theirs to sell or trade. Rather, it was temporarily in their care. As European settlements grew and spread, clashes with Native Americans became more frequent.

1513: the Spaniard Ponce de León explores Florida and encounters the Timucua people, known for their **tattooed** bodies

1539–1543: the Spaniard Francisco Vázquez de Coronado travels through the American southwest, encountering Pueblo tribes

1565: Spanish colonists build the first permanent European settlement on the North American mainland at St Augustine, Florida

This 16th-century engraving shows a European interpretation of the Timucua people living in Florida at the time of European arrival. We can see the unique hairstyles and ear jewellery worn by the Timucua, their housing structures, and a method of cooking.

Furthermore, European diseases devastated tribal populations, which had never had a chance to develop resistance to smallpox, whooping cough, and measles. These diseases wiped out entire communities. Weakened by disease, and faced with European weapons of war such as horses and guns, the power of Native Americans in these regions was broken.

1607: English colonists establish a settlement called Jamestown, Virginia, an area already lived in by the Powhatan Indians

1608: French colonists establish a settlement in Quebec, Canada, and trade with the Huron Indians

1620: English colonists arrive in Massachusetts, where they look to local tribes for help in understanding their new surroundings

Independence from Great Britain

In 1783, Great Britain's colonies in North America won their independence and the United States of America was born. Hungry for land, settlers moved westward. Tribes resisted and adapted to this invasion in various ways.

At this time, the Iroquois confederation – the Seneca, Onondaga, Cayuga, Oneida, Mohawk, and Tuscarora tribes – dominated the northeastern woodlands. Strong because of their unity, numbers, and relatively inland location, they had resisted advancing white settlers in the east for more than 150 years. The Iroquois had developed a government in which all member tribes were represented. In fact, their system of government was later looked to by the **Founding Fathers** of the USA for guidance and inspiration. But during the **American Revolution**, four of the tribes fought with the British, while the Oneida and the Tuscarora sided with the colonists. As a result, the confederation was weakened and it broke apart.

The tribes of the eastern woodlands were almost destroyed after the Revolution. In 1784, the Iroquois were forced to **cede** large parcels of land. In 1813, the Shawnee chief Tecumseh – who had created an **unprecedented** alliance of tribes that fought against the settlers – was killed and his people were pushed out of the Ohio River valley.

This scene, painted in 1881 by Lakota Chief Red Horse, shows warriors riding into battle at the Battle of Little Bighorn.

The Cherokee, Creek, Seminole, Chickasaw, and Choctaw lived in the southeast. They were called the 'five civilized tribes' by white settlers, as many tribal members married white settlers and adopted some of their ways of life. The Cherokee, for example, created courts and developed a written language. The 'five civilized tribes' signed treaties with the settlers, but the settlers ignored the treaties and the tribes were eventually forced to leave their land. At different times during the period 1820 to 1838, the various 'five civilized tribes' were forced to walk almost 1000 miles to Oklahoma along a route bitterly remembered as the Trail of Tears.

1775–83: the American Revolution ends with the creation of the USA; white settlers move further west

1838: most southeastern tribes are forced to move from their homes onto **reservations**; some Seminoles hide in Florida swamplands and elude US soldiers

1870s–80s: Plains Indians are forced to surrender their land and move to reservations

10

The Plains tribes fought hard against white expansion. They were ironically aided by a European import – horses. Mounted on these swift animals, the tribes could fight and hunt much more effectively than they could on foot. But by the late 1870s, buffalo herds had been devastated by white hunters, and the remaining Native Americans were forced onto reservations – pieces of land often far from their original homes.

Recent Native American history

In the second half of the 20th century, Native Americans began to gain a greater voice in North America. They protested and demonstrated in public to demand **redress** and acknowledgement of past wrongs.

Today, Native American populations have increased, tribes govern themselves, and artists continue to create both traditional and new works of art.

Native Americans often look to their past for guidance, but they also live very much in the present. Much of present-day Native American art may be rooted in past traditions, but it can be created using modern tools and techniques, and therefore reflect the problems and triumphs of modern life.

Gerrit Greve painted *Native American War Bonnet* in 1975.

1960s: new activism in Native American communities leads to celebrations of culture and demonstrations against past wrongs

1990: the Native American Arts and Crafts Act of 1990 is passed in the USA and prohibits individuals from advertising art as Native American-made if it is not

2004: The National Museum of the American Indian opens on the National Mall in Washington, DC

11

Beliefs and traditions

Despite different experiences and cultures, Native Americans share the view that all things have a spirit – trees, animals, and people. Native American artists take this spiritual dimension into account when they produce pieces of art.

The spirit world

Native American people have always been concerned about their relationship with the spirit world. They use ceremonies, **rituals**, and prayers to honour and make contact with spirits, to offer thanks, and to live a balanced, respectful life.

Native American art is often filled with images of animals and natural forces – these images call upon the spirits and make ordinary objects **sacred**. For example, hunters and warriors prayed for the power, strength, and speed of the buffalo. A painting of a buffalo could be a way of connecting with the buffalo's spirit, and a way to ask that spirit for help and protection. Some traditional Native American stories tell of how, in ancient times, humans and animals could change into each other at will. Humans often called upon their animal ancestors for aid or advice.

Traditionally, Native American history was told through dance, storytelling, and art. For example, this 19th-century blanket shows the Navajo **creation myth**, in which two sacred beings bring the gift of corn to the Navajo people.

Totem poles, made by the tribes of the northwestern United States and southwestern Canada, are tall structures carved from wood. Totem poles helped different **clans** tell the stories of their ancestors.

Many Native American rituals are a retelling of a sacred story. A ceremony with masks and figures might explain where people came from or how certain animals or plants became the main source of food for a tribe. The stories were also lessons which revealed how a person should act, and advised which spirits were helpful and which should be feared.

Native American art helps bring ancient stories into the contemporary world. For example, the thunderbird – a common image in Native American cultures – is said to cause thunder when it flaps its enormous wings. When it opens its eyes, jagged lightning flashes. Warriors paint the thunderbird on their shields and garments, hoping that the power of the bird will come to their aid in battle.

Healing

Stories are also important in Native American healing ceremonies, as they explain how a person received healing powers. During a ceremony, these powers are called upon to heal a sick person. Masks, charms, and jewellery are important tools, used to draw upon the powers of the spirit world. Healers shake rattles and make paintings to satisfy or drive out the spirits that cause illness.

Native American creation stories

Different Native American nations tell different **creation stories**, but some stories share common themes. One type of shared story, known as an Earth-Diver story, describes the Universe as first being a giant sea. Then a duck or other bird scrapes mud from the bottom of the ocean, and puts the mud on the back of another animal, usually a turtle. The land grows and grows, becoming the Earth. Many Native American nations say that earthquakes come from the movements of the turtle.

Rock art

Native Americans created designs, paintings, and carvings on rocks all over North America – it is estimated that there are at least 15,000 such sites. Some images show designs and shapes. Others depict people and animals. The images are either carved into the rock or painted using different colours of dye. It can be difficult to date the images, or to find out why they were made.

Coming of age

Some rock art has been linked to rites that mark a young person's coming of age. For example, in what is today British Columbia, Canada, young Native Americans went through an important **ritual** to become an adult.

Each boy went into the hills alone. After **fasting**, he prayed to a spirit for a vision that would become his guardian and helper for the rest of his life. The helper might be an animal, such as an eagle or a bear, or it could be a natural force – perhaps sunlight or thunder. After the boy's vision had occurred, he would go to a place among the rocks and paint the vision on a stone surface.

For a girl to become a woman, she was placed alone in a hut. There, she spent time in quiet **contemplation** and performed rituals of tasks that she would have to complete for the rest of her life. When she had finished, she painted images of these tasks on a rock.

Hunting

Rock art often depicted animals. The artists may have believed the images would help them attract and catch their prey. By depicting mythical beings, such as the water panther or the thunderbird, the hunter requested their aid.

Animal rock art often is found along major animal **migration** routes. Images of buffalo are located next to cliffs where hunters drove them to their deaths. Along the northwest coast, there are rock carvings of salmon, a common northwestern fish.

These two figures, which may represent spirits or ancestors, were probably carved into stone by Native Americans hundreds of years ago.

Historic events

Rock art also recorded important historic events. One example, in the Canyon del Muerto in Arizona, shows a figure on horseback with a cross. This symbolizes the arrival of the Spanish and their religion – Christianity.

The existence of rock art such as this is very important for our understanding of history. While we have written accounts from the Spaniards describing their conquest of parts of North America, the rock art created by Native Americans gives us a glimpse into how they themselves viewed the arrival of Europeans and the changing world around them.

Cave paintings

Among the peaks of the Santa Ynez Mountains in present-day California, colourful paintings and designs cover the walls of a cave that was probably a **sacred** space. The images may have been painted by Native American medicine men as long as 400 years ago. Many of the designs are a mystery, but historians believe that one – a black circle outlined in a ring of blazing white – represents the solar **eclipse** that took place on 24 November 1677.

Chumash artists created detailed images for sacred spaces, such as the ones seen here in the Chumash Cave, California.

Land art

Native Americans often sculpted their landscape. More than 3000 years ago, tribes in the eastern woodlands buried their leaders in log-lined tombs constructed below ground. They heaped earth on top of each tomb to form a mound, and the practice spread to other cultures.

The most spectacular mound sculpture to survive depicts a writhing serpent, which is 400 metres (1312 feet) long. The mound's great size indicates that the people who made it – the Hopewell – were a sophisticated people with an organized culture. The Great Serpent Mound in Ohio spirals outward – a rippling body that ends with open jaws about to eat what appears to be an egg.

Many believe the mound symbolized an important religious principle for its builders.

Other cultures inscribed images of figures into the landscape using coloured stones. In Eatonton, Georgia, between 1000 BCE and 1000 CE, Native Americans gathered white quartz boulders to create a giant eagle-shaped figure on the ground.

Medicine wheels

On the plateaux of the eastern Rocky Mountains, collections of rock patterns have been placed on the ground. From above, they look like giant wheels. Huge circles of stones encircle smaller piles of rocks at the centre. Several lines of stones

The Great Serpent Mound in Adams County, Ohio, writhes across the landscape. Some people believe the object in the snake's mouth may be an egg, seen in the upper-right-hand corner. Others think it might be the sun, and that the mound represents night or an **eclipse**.

This medicine wheel is in Sedona, Arizona. Circles represent teachings about life and death. Native Americans still visit the wheels for inspiration and sometimes leave behind mementos and gifts.

radiate from the centres to the outer circles, just like the spokes of a wheel. These designs are called medicine wheels.

Eighty medicine wheels have been discovered in an area that ranges across present-day Wyoming, USA and Alberta, Canada. No one knows exactly what the wheels were used for or when they were laid out. Some historians believe they are 500 years old. Others estimate that they have been there for over 2000 years.

Each medicine wheel may have been a **sacred** spot for the Native Americans who constructed them. Circles are an important symbol in many cultures. The circle has no beginning or end and

embodies the belief common among many Native American tribes that even though each person is born and dies, life itself never ends.

Native Americans may have used medicine wheels as places to seek visions. It is possible that after a period of **fasting** and **contemplation**, people would go to a medicine wheel and seek contact with or messages from the spirits.

Another theory is that medicine wheels were ancient **astronomical** centres. The stones may have been laid out to document sunrises and sunsets during the year, or the wheels may have been basic calendars that kept track of the winter and summer **solstices**.

Architecture

Native Americans built a wide range of structures. Some lived in villages of solid brick or log structures, while others lived in temporary shelters that could be set up or taken down in minutes. All structures were built using local materials that the builders could obtain easily.

Lodges

The Native Americans who lived in the northwestern United States and southwestern Canada moved about far less than the Plains tribes because they had plentiful and reliable supplies of food. Shellfish could be plucked from the Pacific Ocean, while every year the rivers and streams were choked with giant salmon swimming upstream to spawn.

To build their homes, these peoples chopped down giant cedar trees from the surrounding forests, split the logs into planks, and built wooden lodges along the seashore. Each lodge housed a family group, called a **clan**.

On the northern Pacific coast, Native Americans built giant lodges from large planks of cedar. This lodge is a reconstruction of one made by the Haida people on Queen Charlotte Island, Canada.

In a row of lodges, the position of each was determined by rank, with the most powerful clan occupying the place of honour. The lodges were decorated with giant carvings and paintings. These demonstrated the history and power of the clan.

Earth structures

The Mississippian cultures lived in Cahokia, near what is today the city of St Louis, Missouri, from about 800 to 1600 CE. They erected massive earth structures that today survive as towering grass-covered mounds. One mound is approximately 330 metres (1083 feet) long, 215 metres (705 feet) wide, and 30 metres (98 feet) high – more than three times the size of an American football field. Settlers were mystified when they saw these mounds in the 1800s. Today, historians believe they were used for religious ceremonies or as temples for priests. The Mississippian cultures also built mounds that still exist in Oklahoma, Alabama, and Georgia.

The Hopewell people began erecting giant earthen structures in geometric shapes around 500 CE. One such structure, in present-day Newark, Ohio, includes a vast circle of earthen walls connected to form an **octagon**. Several other shapes cover an area of about ten square kilometres (four square miles). It is believed that these geometric structures were used for **astronomical** purposes.

This teepee is a recreation of the type of teepee that would have been used by the Plains Indians.

Teepees

The Plains Indians lived **nomadic** lives on the grassy plains, following the giant buffalo herds that provided them with food, clothing, and shelter. They lived in tent-like structures called **teepees**, which enabled them to move about quickly.

Teepees were made of buffalo skin stretched over a cone of wooden poles. A flap at the top of the teepee provided a hole through which smoke could escape. The teepee was a remarkable structure. It protected people from the harsh winds, cold temperatures, driving rains, and snow of the Great Plains, yet it could be taken down, strapped to a dog or pony's back, and hauled away in a very short time.

Pueblos

In the southwestern USA and northern Mexico, Native Americans lived in buildings made from **adobe** bricks that were dried in the sun and smeared with mud. Spanish explorers later called them pueblos, or 'little villages'. The Spanish also called the tribes who lived there the Pueblos. Today, the tribes that live in this area are **collectively** referred to as the Pueblo tribes.

Each structure in the pueblo was connected to the next, forming a vast interconnected village. Pueblos were built, lived in, and then sometimes abandoned. Mesa Verde (Spanish for 'green table') in Colorado was inhabited from 600 to 1300 CE. Today, **archaeologists** believe that Pueblo societies were under pressure because of **drought**, which made it difficult to grow crops. Also, the threat of war – brought on by competition for scarce resources – forced the Pueblo people to settle in areas that could be easily defended, such as in the crevices and shadows of giant cliffs.

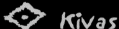 **Kivas**

The wide spaces of the southwestern desert offer few opportunities for concealment. As a result, the Native Americans of this area created their own sacred space in chambers called kivas. These structures, which could be rectangular or circular, were usually set into the ground and covered with logs.

In Chaco Canyon, in northwestern New Mexico, the Anasazi people built a giant pueblo, later called Pueblo Bonita – 'pretty village' – by the Spanish. This village, which flourished between 900 and 1100 CE, had more than 600 rooms and several giant **kivas** – chambers for **sacred** ceremonies. Pueblo Bonita was abandoned around 1150 CE, probably because of drought. By 1300, all of the great pueblos had been abandoned. The Pueblo people scattered throughout the southwest, where their descendants live to this day.

This pueblo, built into the side of a cliff at Mesa Verde, shows the defensive architecture of many pueblos built around 1200 CE. The houses were interconnected and constructed from adobe brick.

Inuit structures

While the tribes of the southwest built pueblos that suited the dry landscape, other Native Americans lived on the northern edges of North America. For at least half the year, the frozen land was in darkness, covered with snow and ice. There, the Inuit people created several structures to cope with this harsh environment.

Igloos were rarely used as permanent dwellings. However, they did provide temporary shelter during hunts and were very effective at sheltering people from the cold and wind.

The Inuit spent the coldest months of the year in wooden structures that were mostly covered in snow. When they left the structure – usually to hunt – they did so through a tunnel. In summer, when the sun shone for most of the day and night, the Inuit lived in tents made from animal skins.

The children of Iqaluit, in the Canadian Northwest Territories, participate in an igloo-building contest as part of the Toonik Tyme Festival. Igloos built of ice blocks were temporary structures, used mostly by hunters seeking shelter overnight. Sealed off from the wind and snow, they trapped body heat. Inside, despite the icy walls, the air is actually quite warm.

Body art

European settlers marvelled at the elaborate art the Native Americans used to decorate their bodies. Paints, dyes, and **tattoos** transformed their skin into a vivid **collage** of symbols. Though many of these decorations were intended to impress, they also served valuable functions. Images of animals, spirits, and mythological beings were believed to bring power to the person wearing them. Symbols said much about the wearer, indicating their rank or stage in life and recounting their feats and exploits.

Chief Four Bears

An excellent example of body art can be seen in this painting of Four Bears – a chief of the Mandan tribe who lived on the Great Plains in the 19th century. The chief's arms are marked with yellow slashes, each one representing a victory over an opponent in hand-to-hand combat. On his chest is a yellow handprint, indicating that he has captured prisoners. Anyone who saw the chief would immediately recognize that he was both a leader and a formidable warrior.

This painting of Mandan chief Four Bears was created by the European painter Karl Bodmer, who travelled among the Plains tribes in the 1830s. Bodmer's paintings show Plains Indian life just before large numbers of European settlers arrived.

Body paint

Many Native Americans covered their bodies in elaborate paint before a special hunt or battle. The patterns and designs had specific meanings. Body paint was also an important part of many ceremonies, like coming-of-age **rituals**, when most young warriors went alone on a **vision quest**. Through **fasting** and hardship, they sought a message or symbol from the spirits that would protect and guide them throughout their lives. Afterwards, warriors called on these spirits using body paint and songs.

Northwestern body art

The Native Americans from the northwestern USA were especially concerned with rank and status in society. Tattoos or body paint were used to identify **clans**. Some men would cover their faces with the shape of an octopus, bear tracks, a killer whale, or even the mouth of a sea monster.

Tattoos were also signs of beauty. Among the Haida tribe, tattoos on a woman's chin were considered very attractive. Tattoos could also be functional. Some members of the Yurok tribe traded with strings of highly valued **dentalium shells**. To check the length of the strings, they held them against their arms, where the lengths and their corresponding values were tattooed.

The Kwakiutl tribe practised a type of body art that involved shaping the skull. The heads of infants were placed between two boards, and then the soft bones of the skull were gently squeezed. Over time, this resulted in a more pointed head, which was considered to be elegant. This process did not harm the child's brain.

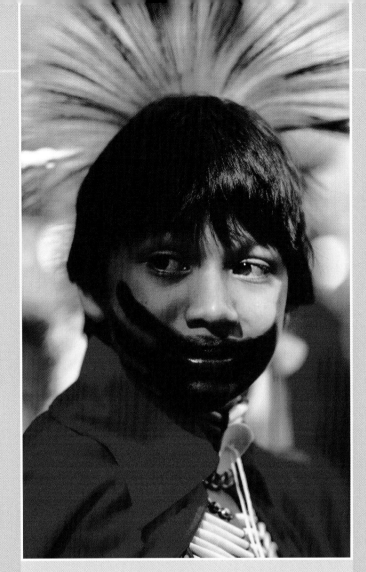

This Native American boy is wearing paint on his face at a modern-day **powwow**. The handprint design shown here is **sacred** to Native Americans, who believe it provides protection against evil spirits.

◈ Horse paint

Native American warriors on the Great Plains did not just paint themselves – they painted their horses, too. Calling on the same spirit powers they asked to protect themselves, warriors covered their horses with designs and colours for battle. The ritual shows the deep love and respect they felt for their mounts.

Clothing, hairstyles, and decoration

Native Americans considered their outward appearance very carefully. For special occasions they wore elaborate headdresses, clothing with intricate beaded patterns, and gleaming pieces of jewellery.

Native American men usually wore a type of leggings or a **loincloth** – this gave them the mobility they needed to hunt or fight. In the summer heat, they remained bare-chested. Women, who farmed or gathered nuts and berries in most Native American cultures, usually wore skirts or dresses.

Hair

Tribal peoples often decorated and styled their hair. Hair was cut into patterns, teased into spikes, and dyed different colours. As with many aspects of Native American culture, each detail and decoration had a meaning.

In the southwest, a hairstyle could indicate whether a woman was of marriageable age. Warriors of the Huron tribe, who lived in what is today eastern Canada, shaved half their head to show that they were fighting men. Tribes detained by the US Army often were forced to cut their hair and then were moved to **reservations**. Native American youths who were sent to boarding schools also were forced to cut their hair. Some Native Americans are taught that their hair is similar to the flowing grasses that are the hair of Mother Earth, and therefore should not be cut. By not permitting these tribes to wear their hair in traditional styles, the US government took away an important part of their culture.

◆ Outside influences

Native American artists were quick to take inspiration from outsiders. Some Plains Indians liked the clothes worn by the US Army so much that after they were presented with officers' uniforms, they used them in their ceremonies. Settlers also learned from Native Americans. For example, settlers in the southwest copied Native American jewellery patterns.

These Native Americans, photographed on a southeastern Idaho reservation in 1897, show some of the elaborate hairstyles and decorations that were worn for a special occasion. Both have woven their hair into two long braids. They have also placed **porcupine roaches** on the tops of their heads, a type of headdress still worn by some men as **regalia** today.

24

Headdresses

Plains Indians often wore feathers in their hair, but these feathers were not random – just one headdress could recount an entire history. For example, an upright feather with a small strip of horsehair indicated that the wearer had won one victory in close fighting. A red feather showed that the wearer had been wounded. A feather with a red dot meant that the wearer had killed a foe. A red feather with bands indicated that the wearer was wounded but that he had also killed enemies – each band signified one kill. A split feather showed that the wearer had been seriously wounded. A feather with a jagged edge told of four victories in close fighting.

This headdress was worn by an Arapaho chief to show his tribe's power and honour. The headdress is made from eagle tail feathers. The eagle was a symbol of strength and spirituality, because it soars higher into the heavens than all other birds.

Jewellery

Almost all Native Americans wore some kind of jewellery. Early **indigenous** peoples wore pieces fashioned from bone, animal claws, or shells. In the northwest, tribes traded coloured **abalone** shells from southern California. These were brighter than northwestern shells, and became popular as pendants among northwestern tribes.

Ancient Native American metalwork tends to be rare. Few tribes had needed to perfect the process necessary to **extract** metal from **ore** because other substances, such as wood or stone, were sufficient for their needs. However, some ancient metal **artefacts** have been discovered in the Great Lakes region and in ancient mounds.

Ancient Mississippi

Native Americans living in the Mississippi River valley from about 1200 to 1450 CE wore several different kinds of jewellery. Ear spools – thick hoops made from stone, pottery, or copper – were worn on the ear and were a sign of elite status. Ear spools were often decorated with a pattern of shapes or grooves. The Mississippian cultures also wore earplugs made from shell, stone, or wood covered with copper. They were worn through the earlobe, like modern earrings.

The Mississippian cultures were very powerful, using war to spread their influence. They used flat sheets of copper to depict images from their culture. One piece depicts a warrior gripping a weapon in one hand and holding a severed head in the other.

Southwestern jewellery

During the last 200 years, southwestern tribes have created some of the finest metal craftwork in North America. After learning how to make silver jewellery in the 1800s, their first examples usually followed native Mexican forms and designs. Although many tribes have developed unique jewellery styles, designs today are often based on ancient stone carvings or motifs from Pueblo ceremonies or religion. A jewellery maker cuts a design from a flat piece of silver. Then, parts of the jewellery are often treated to make them turn black, providing a dramatic contrast to the silver's sheen.

Modern Pueblo jewellery artists follow old traditions but use new methods to produce artworks. Here, Leo Tewa Coriz is **soldering** a silver pendant in his workshop.

This turquoise and silver bracelet was made by Pueblo artist Leo Tewa Coriz in 1995.

Turquoise

Turquoise was considered **sacred** by southwestern tribes. It is often used as the centrepiece in beautiful silver settings. Turquoise can be found in an array of blues and greens. This type of jewellery is now very popular throughout the world.

◈ Dance sticks

In the 1800s, Plains Indians carried **coup** sticks into battle. If a warrior touched an enemy with one of these sticks, he achieved a deed of great bravery, known as a coup. In the 20th century, coup sticks became more and more decorated.

Today known as dance sticks, they are common objects at **powwows**. The staffs taken to powwows are actually the original flags of the indigenous nations. They are highly revered and handled with great care.

Carving

The Native Americans of the northwest, such as the Kwakiutl and Tlingit peoples, were expert carvers. Large forests grew throughout the region, and the tribes that lived there used wood for their shelters and their art. Some carvings, such as pipes, were small enough to fit in your hand. Others, like **totem poles**, were tall, brightly painted structures.

Totem poles

On strips of beach between the forests and the Pacific Ocean, northwestern tribes erected villages of wooden lodges. In front of each lodge stood at least one totem pole. Carved from giant cedar trees, the largest poles towered over the settlement. The carvings were of creatures such as grizzly bears, birds, killer whales, and humans. These totem poles were not just art objects for the people who created them. They told the story of each **clan**, its status and rank, and **commemorated** its dead.

Carving a totem pole

Carvers from northwestern tribes could devote almost all their time to their work. With ready access to abundant supplies, the efforts of the entire tribe were not needed to gather food.

The carver first selected a good cedar tree – a tree that was soft enough to carve, but durable and resistant to the wet climate. After the tree was cut, hollowed out, and dragged to the village, the carving began.

Totem poles were many different sizes. Some were only 3 metres (9.8 feet) tall; others could reach heights of more than 15 metres (49 feet). Some totem poles were covered with brightly coloured paints as well as carvings.

Storytelling

A typical totem pole told an intricate story that explained a clan's origins and powers. These stories were a part of the **oral tradition** of a tribe, clan, or family, and were passed down from generation to generation.

Like many other Native Americans, those in the northwest believed that in ancient times, animals could change into people. Most clans therefore had an animal ancestor, such as a grizzly bear or a wolf. To represent this on the totem pole, the carvers might show a bear protectively holding the symbol of the clan in its paws. If an animal, such as a bear, had helped an ancient ancestor of the clan, this might be symbolized by a human figure crouched behind the bear's legs. If the story involved a wolf, a figure might be shown clinging to the animal's tail. If a totem pole showed a bear with a figure trapped in its jaws, this symbolized the victory over an ancient enemy.

Totem poles were sunk into the sand on the beach, facing outward. This meant that anyone approaching from the ocean – for example, paddling in a canoe – would know exactly where to land.

This magnificent totem pole, which stands on the harbourfront at Victoria, British Columbia, Canada, captures the grizzly bear's snarling expression. Grizzly bears inspired respect and fear among the northwestern Native Americans.

Ritual masks

Native Americans created masks for ceremonies and **rituals**. The masks depicted people, animals, spirits, or natural forces. However, masks had different purposes in different places. In the southwest, a person wearing a mask transformed into the spirit which that mask represented. In the Arctic, masks were essential for hunting and healing rituals.

Inuit masks

In what is today Alaska, Native Americans produced some of the most vivid masks of all. The masks were used in ceremonies designed to ensure a successful hunt. Starvation was never far away in the icy Arctic, so these masks were considered extremely important.

These Native Americans, mostly members of the Inuit tribe, believe that everything has an inner spirit – called an *inua*. Their masks show the outer and inner spirits of each creature. One half of a mask might depict an animal, such as a seal, while the other half might show a human-like face, representing the animal's *inua*. A dancer would wear the mask in special dances and rituals that were intended to show respect to the spirit of the seal. The Inuit people hoped the seal would return the gesture of respect by allowing itself to be killed.

Shamans wore special masks during healing ceremonies. These masks could be truly amazing, with a tiny smiling face, feathers, and sticks poking out. By wearing such a mask, the shaman asked for the powers and help of the spirit world to cure an illness.

Transformation masks like this one were used by many northern tribes such as the Haida. The masks were opened at appropriate moments in a dance to reveal different aspects of the figure the dancer was impersonating. This wooden thunderbird mask is opened to reveal a human face, expressing both the human and animal nature of the spirits.

This mask represents the mythical figure Bokwus – the Kwakiutl Wild Man of the Woods and chief of the dead. According to the myth, Bokwus lived in the forests of the northwest, feeding on rotten wood and grubs. He offered what appeared to be dried salmon to people chancing upon him, but after tasting the salmon they died and joined his ghostly followers.

Masks from the northwest

When winter blanketed the northwest coast in freezing mists, the Tlingit tribe moved inland. They lived off stores of food that had been collected during the summer. It was a time for important ceremonies, dances, and festivals, and masks played an essential role.

In the flickering light of a lodge fire, masked dancers reenacted stories. Some recounted the stories of the clan's ancestors. Others depicted dark spirits engaged in evil or destructive actions, such as a sea monster that was said to cause floods and lead canoes astray. Other masks showed good spirits of people, animals, or nature.

The masks could be very dramatic and complex – some could even be worked by strings, swinging open and shut to show the transformation of a person or spirit into an animal and back again. Other masks had several interchangeable mouthpieces that were designed to produce different sound effects and voices. Actors wore masks as they delivered their lines. These often included moveable features such as eyebrows and lips.

Today, ceremonies continue to be practised in the northwest. Many masks have been conserved from the past and are still used today.

Kachinas

In the southwest, it is said that spirits called **kachinas** came out of the mountains every year to visit tribal peoples. Kachinas are spirits – of rain, clouds, the dead, gods, and goddesses. There are several hundred kachinas in Pueblo culture, some guaranteeing a safe home, others rain, and a good crop. Some represent good or angry spirits, while others are simply clowns who entertain the people. Some kachinas are universal characters familiar to all Pueblo peoples, while others are only believed in by certain clans.

Each kachina has its own distinct mask. Native Americans dress in these masks and decorate their bodies to perform dances in underground chambers called **kivas**. In these ceremonies, the masks allow the spirits of the kachinas to enter the bodies of the dancers. Some kachinas brought medicine and healing powers, others controlled the seasons, while others blessed new homes. This ensured that the powers of the spirits would benefit the community for at least another year, at which time the ceremonies would be repeated.

This kachina doll, created in the 1850s by a Hopi artist in the American southwest, represents a rain spirit. Rain was needed to grow the corn depended on by southwestern tribes. Here, the kachina's eyes depict clouds of rain and the eyelashes are raindrops.

Kachina dolls

Pueblo artists made kachina dolls for younger members of the tribe. These dolls were important learning tools. They were used to teach young Pueblos many complex stories of the kachina spirits and the traditions of their culture. Standing 15 to 30 centimetres (6 to 12 inches) tall, they are elaborately decorated and painted.

Today, Native American artists in the southwest continue to carve Kachina dolls. Their styles have evolved over time. Modern Native American artists usually carve the kachina from a single piece of wood, which they then decorate with paint, rather than making separate items for the doll to wear. The decoration of clothing takes its inspiration from modern society – some kachina dolls wear T-shirts. Many people of different cultures are interested in these dolls, and they often sell for large sums of money.

These modern kachina dolls represent several characters and spirits. The headdresses, body paint, masks, and tools identify each individual kachina and its powers. It is likely that these dolls were made to be sold.

◈ Learning tools

Southwestern Native Americans protected their culture by not sharing many **artefacts** or stories about their ceremonies. Photographs of their rituals are rare, and they hardly ever allow someone from outside their village to observe **sacred** ceremonies in kivas. However, a little has been learnt about kachina dress and ceremonies through kachina dolls.

33

Stone carving

Some Native Americans, notably those from the Hopewell culture in the eastern woodlands, considered stone carvings to be important enough to bury with their dead. Some tribes still follow this practice today. Most of the Hopewell carvings show animals taking part in a variety of activities. For example, one shows a bird spearing a fish with its beak, while another is in the shape of a beaver chipping away at a tree trunk. The carvings reveal not only artistic skill but also a keen appreciation of how wild animals act. This realism made the objects more effective in their purpose – to invoke the spirits to come to the aid of the dead person with whom they were buried.

The Inuit often made pipes from animal bone, covering them with designs and carvings of animals and people.

Pipe carving

The Hopewell people devoted enormous artistic energy to carving pipes from stone. Smoking was never done simply for pleasure or relaxation. Tobacco was a highly valuable substance that was offered to the spirits and smoked at ceremonies – the wafting smoke was considered to unite the spirit world with the earthly world. Pipes were signs of peace and union with the spirit world and, as such, were covered with images reflecting this importance. Hopewell pipes were usually carved in the shape of an animal such as a frog, a hawk, or a panther. Freshwater pearls were often set into the head as eyes. Some rituals and ceremonies relied on the act of sharing a pipe in order to call on the spirit world.

The pipe was also extremely important among Plains tribes. There, pipes were considered not just a bridge to the spirit world, but also a link to past generations. According to Lakota teachings, the pipe was a gift from the Creator.

This Hopewell pipe, carved from stone between 300 BCE and 500 CE, was originally buried in a mound tomb. The Hopewell often carved animal shapes into their pipes.

It is said that a beautiful spirit called White Buffalo Calf Woman presented the pipe to the Lakota with these words:

"Behold this pipe! Remember always how sacred it is and treat it as such, for it will take you to the end. Remember, in me there are four ages. I am leaving but will look back on your people in every age, and in the end I will return."

Modern pipes

Native American artists continue to carve pipes to this day. White Buffalo Calf Woman's words have been remembered and the pipe is still seen in ceremonies among the Lakota and other tribes. The Plains Indians often decorate their pipes. Just as they cover clothing or shields with images, these tribes also use objects – such as pipes – to tell their own histories. The pipe makes the power of each group's images and objects come alive and enter the living world.

Pottery

Native American cultures throughout North America made pottery to store and cook food and to carry water. Some cultures decorated these pots or moulded them into figures. The Mississippi culture, for example, created several pots in the shape of human faces or figures. Wherever pottery was made, it was created from local clay, shaped by hand, and heated by fire until it became hard.

This water **pitcher** was created almost 1000 years ago by the southwestern Mogollon culture. It is a fine example of the spiral paint patterns that the Mogollon favoured.

Coil pots

The firing and painting of pottery flourished in the southwest, where techniques and patterns were passed from generation to generation for centuries. Native American potters in this area still use traditional materials and methods today. These potters dig clay from the local mesas – mountains with flat summits and steep sides. The clay is moulded into long flat tubes that are then coiled into the shape of a pot or bowl. The sides are then smoothed over.

Once a piece was formed, it was painted with natural colours – for example, black paint was made by boiling a plant called beeweed. The paint was applied with a brush made from the leaves of the yucca plant. Instead of hardening the pot in a **kiln**, the potters set it over a fire made from goat dung. There was very little wood in the southwest and goat dung heated quickly and evenly.

Mimbres pottery

The Mimbres culture, which flourished in the southwest between 1000 and 1200 CE, produced pottery with painted designs. These designs mostly showed local animals, such as beetles, birds, jackrabbits, antelope, and coyotes.

In the Mimbres culture, it was traditional to put a pottery bowl with a hole in it over the head of a dead person and bury it with them. It was believed that the potter poured his or her soul into the bowl when he or she created it. By creating a hole in the bowl, the person's soul was free to join the dead on the journey to the afterlife.

This modern pot, made in the American southwest, is decorated with a bird design common to the Mimbres tradition.

Anasazi and Pueblo pottery

The Anasazi, meaning 'enemy of our ancient ones', lived from about 1100 to 1450 CE in the southwest. They crafted bowls, drinking pots, and pitchers from clay, usually decorating them with geometric black-and-white designs. When the Anasazi civilization broke apart into various Pueblo tribes, these Native Americans began to produce pottery decorated with colourful designs. By the 1880s, the Pueblo tribes had become known around the world for their pottery.

Modern pottery

Pueblo pottery is still being produced today. In San Ildefonso Pueblo in New Mexico, a husband and wife developed a new way to decorate pottery. They packed each piece with cow dung and held it over a smoky fire. The result was a dark clay that could be decorated with a rich red colour. They continued to produce this pottery throughout the 1970s.

Textiles

Many Native Americans were accomplished weavers, creating designs with great skill and imagination. The textiles they wove were used to make clothing, baskets, and bags.

Navajo weaving

From the 18th century onwards, Native Americans in the southwest used **looms** to create rugs and robes with colourful designs. The Navajo were especially skilful at this craft – they had learned the technique from their Pueblo neighbours. The Navajo used geometric designs and, to provide more colour, they sometimes pulled apart European blankets and wove the thread into their own work.

Towards the end of the 19th century, the Navajo began creating new designs. Some of the patterns reflected the local environment, for instance, a flat desert landscape broken only by giant mesas. The patterns also signified status, with chiefs wearing richly decorated robes.

The weaving was – and still is – usually done by women. There are more than 30,000 Navajo weavers today, each producing unique pieces. Recently, they have begun to use more modern dyes and colours, such as pastels, to sell to tourists, but they still use ancient patterns. Some patterns include a variety of stripes, while others use spirit motifs or images taken from sand paintings.

Weaving with wood

The northwestern tribes took advantage of their local forests for weaving materials. Roots taken from spruce trees were strong but flexible. Cedar and wild cherry bark were also used. The roots and bark were washed until soft and cut into strips. These strips were then woven into clothing textiles. The bark was water resistant, allowing the wearer to stay dry in the wet climate.

For ceremonial garments, northwestern weavers used wool from mountain goats. The robes and shawls they made followed designs that were carved into **totem poles**. Their beauty made them sought after by the other tribes with whom they traded, who regarded them as symbols of high status and wealth.

This robe was woven from pure goat's wool by a member of the Chilkat tribe. Robes such as these were considered to be extremely valuable and worn only by important people during **sacred** ceremonies. When the wearer died, he or she would be buried in the robe.

38

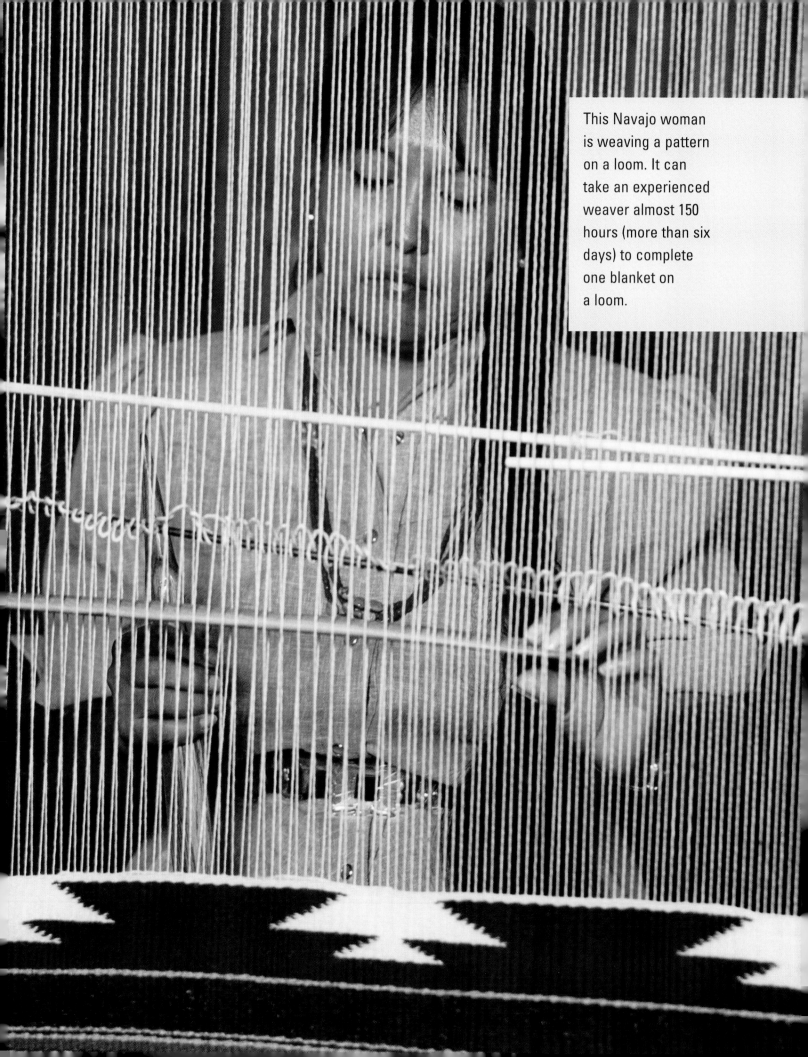

This Navajo woman is weaving a pattern on a loom. It can take an experienced weaver almost 150 hours (more than six days) to complete one blanket on a loom.

Baskets

Baskets were an essential tool as well as an art form. They were used to carry goods, store food, hold infants, and bury the dead. Basket weavers produced exquisitely designed patterns, using many different shapes and decorations. For example, the Anishianabe tribes wove coil baskets from sweetgrass and sewed other baskets from birchbark.

Artistic touches often had a practical use. Tin bells were attached to Apache baskets. The Apache lived in the southwest, an area with many poisonous snakes. When they carried these baskets, the bells warned snakes away. Cherokees used a double-weave pattern that made their baskets very strong. Another basket, made to carry huckleberries, was broad and shallow. Huckleberries are soft, and this design prevented them from being crushed. Skilled Pomo craftsmen from what is today California wove special patterns into baskets. These were meant to be gateways for good spirits to enter the baskets and could be as simple as a single notch in the pattern.

Colourful baskets are both useful objects and decorated works of art in many Native American cultures.

Basket weaving

Basket weavers use four basic techniques – wicker, plaiting, twining, and coiling. Each technique produces a different effect. Weavers use fibres from plants that have been grown and tended for several years. These plants are then harvested and dried, and the stalks are cut into strips using knives, fingernails, or teeth. Just before the weaver starts work, he or she soaks the stalks in water to soften them. The best baskets keep their shape, even after years of use.

A modern craft

In the last few years, basket weaving has again become extremely popular. Several Native American organizations weave baskets and hold exhibitions to display their work. Many organizations are modelled on Native-American basketry groups that flourished at the beginning of the 20th century.

This basket, woven by members of the Pomo tribe, is made from several different materials, including woodpecker, quail, and hummingbird feathers.

Southwestern baskets

Some excellent examples of basket weaving come from the southwestern region of the United States. The Pueblo Indians, who still weave baskets today, use patterns and techniques that date back more than 1000 years.

To make a basket, Pueblo weavers gather local plants. Rabbit brush and sumac are used to weave wicker baskets, while coiled baskets are made mostly from yucca. The plants are wrapped tightly into a coil and dyed different colours, and are then woven into dazzling patterns.

Baskets traditionally fulfilled many essential tasks in tribal life. Peach baskets were used to carry and store fruit. Burden baskets were strapped to animals and used to carry heavy or large objects. Baskets in the shape of flat trays were used to sift cornmeal or to serve piki – a thin bread made from blue cornmeal.

Painting

The Great Plains tribes were among the few Native Americans who painted on flat surfaces, like European painters. They covered buffalo skins with images of people, animals, spirits, and scenes of hunting and war.

Both Native American men and women painted, although their styles differed. Women often produced **abstract** paintings and portrayed sweeping themes, while men opted for more realistic pictures that featured their exploits in war and hunting. They also covered shields with images of animals that would protect them or give them special powers in battle.

Robe paintings

Female Plains Indians decorated buffalo robes with complex designs and patterns. Although the designs might look as if they are made up of simple geometric patterns at first glance, each colour and shape has a meaning. For example, one artist painted a buffalo robe in the late

Winter counts

Plains Indians recorded their history through a 'winter count'. This usually consisted of a buffalo skin decorated with several pictures. Each year an artist added a picture – a painting of the most important events to affect the tribe. Some recorded the efforts of medicine men to increase numbers of buffalo during the 1880s, when white hunters were rapidly slaughtering the great herds. The years after the 1880s were often represented by log cabins, which symbolized a new way of life on the **reservation**.

This winter count was drawn on cotton cloth by a Yanktonai Lakota called Blue Thunder. It records events which took place between 1792–93 and 1902–03. It may show the arrival of white soldiers (note the US soldier dressed in blue, bottom left), or a buffalo hunt (note the buffalo, bottom right).

19th century. In the robe's centre, she placed a rectangle that enclosed several shapes. It is believed that the rectangle symbolized the Earth. A red-and-yellow stripe represented the Sun and the day. Three diamonds inside the rectangle stood for a man, a woman, and animals. A long yellow line through the centre was the Milky Way. Finally, a triangle with a red spot represented a traditional story about six sisters who lived alone because they refused to marry.

Male Plains artists often decorated their robes with scenes from their lives, showing themselves hunting or in battle. These robes, which were worn on special occasions, were meant to impress onlookers. Mandan Chief Mato-Tope, for example, drew himself shooting, spearing, hacking, and knifing opponents, all on a single robe. Lakota warriors also depicted battle scenes on their **teepees**. Some of these homes were covered with figures galloping on horseback into war.

Apart from the Plains Indians, several other tribes painted, though few used animal skin as a canvas. Northwestern tribes decorated their carvings – masks and **totem poles** – with bright-coloured paint to enhance the realistic effect. In the southwest, artists painted **sacred** places for ceremonial purposes and created other 'painted' works using coloured sand and earth.

Colour and detail

Northwestern artists were not satisfied with simply carving a figure. To give it an even more lifelike appearance, they added intricate painted details. Carvings of bear teeth and eyes were coloured white, while ravens were given realistic black beaks. The orca – also known as the killer whale – which swam in the waters along the Pacific coast, was depicted in its distinctive black-and-white pattern. But paint was not just used to reproduce a likeness. Craftsmen also painted designs and **clan** symbols on the animals' figures or, in the case of birds, on their wing feathers.

Northwestern tribes were inspired by the black-and-white patterns of the orcas that swam in the Pacific Ocean. The design on this bright Tlingit blanket, probably decorated in the late 19th century, depicts a killer whale. The artist obtained the blanket through trade with the **Hudson Bay Company**, illustrating the mix of artistic cultures and the use of new materials common at this time.

Sand painting

In the southwest, ceremony and art continue to converge as they have for thousands of years. Sand paintings were and are created by medicine men during healing **rituals**. In some cases, creating an image can take days.

Using different coloured types of soil, sand, clay, and stone, a medicine man creates a picture on the ground. The person who is to be healed sits near the picture, facing toward the east – the source of all blessings – while the medicine man depicts the various spirits that could have caused the illness. The healer hopes the spirits will enter the painting and be pleased by it. If they are pleased, they will reward the healer by curing the sick person. When the painting is finished, the medicine man wipes the area clean. Gathering and preparing the materials used to create the art, as well as the mental and spiritual preparation of the artist, are considered to be an **integral** part of the artistic process.

A Navajo medicine man carefully sprinkles coloured sand onto a sand painting. Sand paintings are still an important healing and cultural ritual among the Navajo today.

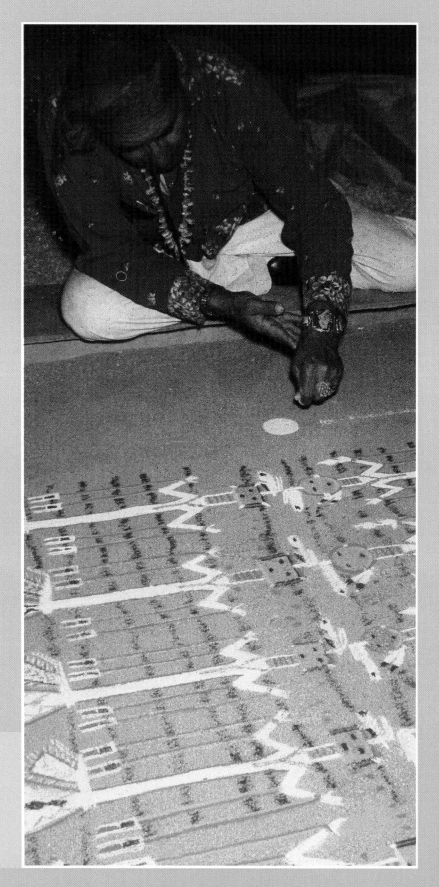

Kiva paintings

Ancient southwestern artists covered the walls of sacred chambers, called **kivas**, with paintings. These images often depicted spirits called **kachinas**, who had a variety of powers, such as helping corn crops to grow. In one painting, a spirit was shown surrounded by the ingredients of life – corn, rainclouds, and sunshine. Others showed kachinas bringing rain. When these paintings were discovered, centuries later, members of the Pueblo tribes recognized the symbols and figures.

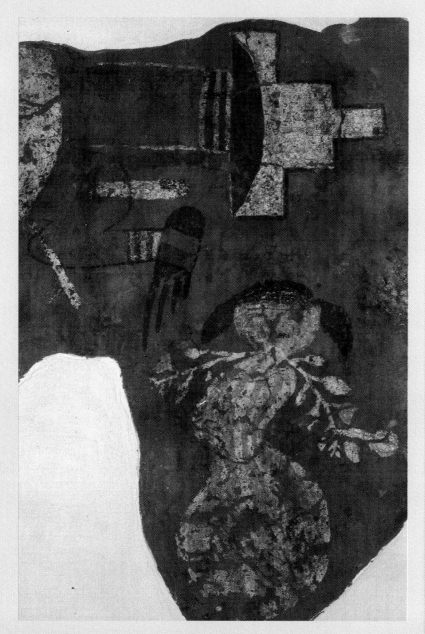

Native American artists of the southwest covered kiva walls with sacred paintings, some of which have survived for centuries. These fragments show a woman dancer holding twigs.

Cutting out paper

Cutting pictures from paper is a traditional craft in some areas of Mexico. In the village of San Pablito Puebla, the Otomi cut the figures of the Spirit of the Tomato and the Spirit of the Banana out of bark paper to encourage their crops to grow. These paper seed spirits are shown holding ripe fruit and vegetables.

A modern craft

In Puebla and Veracruz people cut brightly coloured tissue and metallic paper into intricate designs. A very sharp chisel, a hammer, and a razor are used to mark and cut out the patterns. Then these lacy paper cuttings are hung around the town or used to decorate the outsides of churches on special occasions.

Ceremonies, songs, and dances

Native American tribes throughout North America used ceremonies to mark the change of seasons and to ask the spirits of hunting or **agriculture** for their aid.

Plant celebrations

Vegetation was the main source of food for many Native American tribes. In the southwest, the corn harvest was essential. At the winter **solstice**, the Hopi celebrate their New Year with a special appeal to the corn goddesses. At this time, two female **kachina** spirits – Blue Corn Girl and Yellow Corn Girl – are said to appear to greet the renewal of the Sun.

This robe painting on animal hide depicts the Sun Dance. The painting, which was probably made in the 1880s, also shows the growing presence of white settlers, represented by the cross.

The Sun Dance

The Sun Dance is one of the oldest and most **sacred** ceremonies for the people of the Great Plains. Participants spend months preparing for this dance, which is both a prayer and a sacrifice. Some view the ceremony as a test of strength and courage. During the dance, people offer the only thing they truly possess: their bodies. To perform the dance, a **brave** pierces his chest with **awls** that are connected to a tall pole with straps. He then dances around the pole, tugging on the straps until pieces of flesh are pulled from his body. The Sun Dance was outlawed by white authorities in 1881. However, the dance was practised in secret until 1978, when the Native American Religious Freedom Act was passed in the United States, allowing Native Americans to practise their religions freely.

The Ghost Dance

By the 1880s, most Plains Indians had been forced to move from their homelands to **reservations**. Torn from their traditional ways of life, a new religious belief began to spread. It was called the Ghost Dance and was based upon the vision of Wovoka – a Paiute Indian from Nevada. The Ghost Dance foretold that white settlers would disappear, the buffalo would return, and dead ancestors of the Native Americans would reappear to create a paradise on Earth. Many Plains Indians performed the Ghost Dance in specially decorated garments that they believed would ward off the bullets fired by white soldiers.

In 1890, a group of Ghost Dancers and 300 other Lakota men, women, and children were massacred at Wounded Knee in South Dakota. They were killed by a group of white soldiers who mistakenly thought the dancers had gathered to wage war.

Native Americans participating in the Ghost Dance called upon the power of the thunderbird – a fierce being that caused thunder when it flapped its wings, and flashed lightning when it opened its eyes. By drawing the thunderbird on a piece of clothing such as this robe, the wearer hoped to gain some of the being's power and protection.

Modern powwows are occasions to wear traditionally decorated clothing and to practise traditional dances. The modern powwow has evolved alongside changes in Native American lifestyles and culture, but it has always been a time to be sociable, celebrate, feast, dance, sing, and give thanks.

Powwows

Some tribes, such as the Shawnee of Ohio, broke into smaller groups during the winter. When food was scarce, it was easier to feed a smaller number of people. They joined together again in summer, and this annual event became a special gathering when important issues were discussed, songs and dances were performed, and traditions were reaffirmed. The gathering was called a **powwow** – a term that probably derives from the Algonquin term *pauau*, which describes a gathering of medicine men and leaders for a healing ceremony.

Today, powwows are held throughout the summer in North America. Powwows reaffirm tribal identity and are an important forum for tribes to make and maintain contact with each other.

Powwow ceremonies

There are two main categories of powwows: traditional powwows and contest powwows. During a contest powwow, drum groups and dancers compete for cash prizes. Dances of all kinds are performed at powwows. Dancers wear garments covered in shimmering patterns of beads and colour. The whirling group of dancers is guided by the steady beat of drums and songs.

New kinds of art are displayed at powwows. The art reflects the historical changes Native Americans have experienced. Many of the bead patterns, decorations, and headdresses are a compilation of different tribal customs. It is not unusual to see a dancer wearing a Plains headdress at the same time as a shirt decorated with patterns from the eastern woodlands. This is part of the pan-Native American movement, in which Native Americans from different tribes come together to celebrate and support all Native American traditions. Though some tribe members still feel rivalry with other tribes, most Native Americans recognize themselves as belonging to a larger culture.

Giveaway ceremony

Giveaway ceremonies often take place during powwows. During these ceremonies, members of a community present one another with gifts. A gift can be simple or large, an object of artistry or a basic set of tools. The point is to give thanks to someone for his or her help during a difficult time, or to acknowledge the completion of a person's schooling or military service.

These Ojibwe women, dressed in their **regalia**, are taking part in a dance contest powwow on the Leech Lake Indian Reservation near Cass Lake, Minnesota. Some powwows also have cooking and horseback riding competitions.

◈ A modern tradition

The popularity of powwows has grown enormously in recent times, attracting tourists and Native Americans seeking connections. Native Americans socialize, swap news and stories, renew friendships, and meet new people. They also cook traditional food and make traditional crafts. The powwow is still an important way of living and passing on Native American culture.

Cross-currents

Though early contact between Native Americans and settlers was often marked by destruction and violence, there was also an important artistic exchange between cultures. For example, settlers traded glass beads to Native Americans for fur **pelts**. These beads were often used in Native American clothing patterns, and the settlers used the fur to make coats and hats.

Conserving culture

Interactions between Native Americans and whites have affected each culture's art. For example, in the 19th century, the fur trade between northwestern tribes and whites made those tribes wealthy enough to **commission** giant **totem poles**. However, later that century, most tribes stopped carving them when Canadian authorities declared the practice illegal. Instead, northwestern artists began to make small totem poles for tourists. Then, in the 1930s, the US government hired Alaskan carvers to make copies of poles and raise them in 'totem parks'. This helped keep the carving tradition alive, and in the 1950s the Canadian ban on totem poles was lifted.

The interest in Native American art has continued to grow outside of the Native American population, drawing the attention of scholars and museums. Northwestern artists have been asked by museums and wealthy individuals to carve poles for their collections, for example, and in 2004, a huge new museum dedicated to Native American Art opened on the National Mall in Washington, DC. However, it is important to recognize that not all Native Americans believe that all types of tribal art should be placed in museums.

In 1938, the US Forest Service began hiring master totem pole carvers from northwestern tribes in an attempt to keep this art form from being lost. Carver John Wallace made this totem pole for Totem Bight State Park in Alaska in 1947.

Modern Native American artists

In 1990, the **Indian Arts and Crafts Board** was granted expanded powers of civil and criminal **jurisdiction** over **counterfeit** Native American arts and crafts. The Native American Arts and Crafts Act of 1990 made it illegal for anyone other than a Native American artist to advertise his or her artwork as being Native American, or as belonging to a particular tribe. This act helped establish a place in the art world for genuine Native American art – art that was born of and influenced by a true Native American tradition.

Native Americans have sought to reconnect themselves with their past and use it to guide their lives. Many of these craftspeople use the techniques of their ancestors, although these are sometimes modified. For example, Bill Reid of the Haida tribe uses modern carving tools to depict the ancient stories of the northwestern Native Americans. Norval Morrisseau of the Ojibwe tribe uses modern paints in his scenes of Native American culture. Rick Bartow of the Yurok tribe uses a variety of **media**, including printing, charcoal, and acrylic paints, to create colourful images of transformation. Kay Walkingstick of the Cherokee tribe paints images that incorporate historic Native Americans and the modern world.

The work of these artists and many others gives new life to some of the world's oldest and greatest artistic traditions. Today, the next generation of Native American artists is applying new artistic techniques to tribal histories, documenting the current link in the chain of Native American art and culture.

Today, many Native American artists use modern materials, such as the ink wash in this picture, to show traditional themes. This warrior was created by Gerrit Greve in 1976.

Further resources

More books to read

Brown, Dee, *Bury My Heart at Wounded Knee* (Henry Holt & Co., 1991)

Cassidy, James J, (ed). *Through Indian Eyes: The Untold Story of Native American Peoples* (Reader's Digest, 1995)

Coe, Ralph T, *Sacred Circles: The Indianness of North American Indian Art* (Arts Catalogue of Great Britain, 1976)

Feder, Norman, *Two Hundred Years of North American Indian Art* (Praeger Publishers, 1971)

Hunt, Norman Bancroft, *Native Americans: The Life and Culture of the North American Indian* (Chartwell Books, 1996)

Reynoldson, Fiona, *Living Through History: Native Americans* (Heinemann, 2000)

Zimmerman, Larry J, *American Indians: The First Nations, Native North American Life, Myth and Art* (Duncan Baird Publishers, 2003)

Zimmerman, Larry J, and Brian Leigh Molyneaux, *Native North America* (University of Oklahoma Press, 2000)

Websites

http://www.heard.org/exhibits-current.php
Heard Museum of Native Cultures and Art: Current Exhibitions

http://americanhistory.si.edu/timeline/01pots.htm
National Museum of American History: American Encounters

http://www.nmculture.org
Native American Museums and Monuments of New Mexico

http://www.nativetech.org
Native American Technology and Art

http://www.smithsonian.org/resource/faq/nmai/start.htm
Smithsonian Institution: Native American Resources

http://www.hanksville.org/NAresources/indices/NAmuseums.html
WWW Virtual Library – American Indians
Index of Native American Museum Resources on the Internet

Places to visit

USA

Anasazi Heritage Center, Dolores, Colorado

Aztec Ruins National Monument, Aztec, New Mexico

Cultural Resources Center, Suitland, Maryland

George Gustav Heye Center, New York

Heard Museum of Native Cultures and Art, Phoenix, Arizona

Mashantucket Pequot Museum & Research Center, Mashantucket, Connecticut

Smithsonian National Museum of the American Indian Branches

UK

British Museum, London

Horniman Museum, London

Pitt Rivers Museum, Oxford

Australia

The Four Winds Gallery, Double Bay, NSW

Glossary

abalone   type of mollusc whose shell is lined with mother of pearl, a shiny, multicoloured substance favoured in jewellery

abstract   art that uses shape, colour and pattern to communicate artists' ideas

adapt   get used to something new, such as a climate, physical landscape, or culture

adobe   mud mixed with straw that forms a paste-like substance; this substance dries into a hard material that is used like a modern brick

agriculture   planting and raising of crops in an organized, planned manner

American Revolution   (1775–1783) war fought between Great Britain and her colonies in North America

archaeologist   scientist who studies the physical remains of past cultures

arid   dry; lacking or with very little water

artefact   object made by humans long ago

astronomical   having to do with the study of outer space and celestial bodies such as planets and stars

awls   small, pointed tools

brave   young Native American warrior

cede   surrender possession of

clan   group of people within a larger tribe who are members of the same family

collage   combination of many shapes or images

collectively   as a group

colony   settlement of people who have come from another country to live in a new place

commemorate   honour with a ceremony

commission   place an order for, ask someone to create something (usually an artistic work)

contemplation   thoughtful study

counterfeit   object made to look like something else in an attempt to fool the viewer

coup   a blow or a strike; some tribes were known to 'count coup', to touch an enemy during battle to prove bravery

creation myths   stories that tell how each tribe came to be

creation stories   stories that explain the origins of each Native American group

dentalium shells   mollusc shells, often white and cone shaped

drought   long period of dryness that prevents the growth of crops

eclipse   blocking of the Sun's light by another body, such as a planet

extract   separate metal from ore

fasting   not eating food

Founding Fathers   American statesmen – such as George Washington and Thomas Jefferson – credited with shaping the early years of the USA

game   wild animals hunted for food, such as buffalo

Hudson Bay Company   British company established in 1670 to carry on business in Canada; this company still exists today

Ice Age   period of cold temperatures, when glaciers are present

igloo   structure made from large blocks of ice, usually used by northern tribes as a hunting base

Indian Arts and Crafts Board a government agency created by the US Congress to help Native American communities develop economically through arts and crafts marketing

indigenous belonging to a place

integral absolutely necessary

inua soul believed to exist in each person, animal, plant, lake, and mountain

irrigation supply of water to dry land through a series of connected channels dug in the earth

jurisdiction legal authority to control or make decisions about something

kachinas spirits of Pueblo ancestors

kiln oven used to bake and harden pottery

kiva chamber in a Pueblo village used for ceremonies and meetings

loincloth strip of cloth worn about a man's waist

loom tool used to help weave fabric or thread

media any material used in a work of art

mica rock-forming mineral that flakes easily and was often used in Native American art

migration mass movement of people or animals from one place to another, sometimes on a regular, seasonal basis

nomadic describing people who have no fixed home and move about in search of food

octagon eight-sided shape

oral tradition passing of tribal histories and stories verbally from one generation to the next; a spoken – not written – history

ore mineral containing metal

pelt animal skin with the fur still attached

pitcher container for liquids

porcupine roaches head ornaments made from porcupine hair and worn by male dancers

powwow celebratory gathering of Native American tribes

Puritan member of a group of English Protestants who travelled to the USA in the 17th century

redress make amends for, set right

regalia traditional clothing worn during ceremonies

reservations pieces of land set aside by the US government for Native Americans, often far from the tribes' original homes

rituals religious ceremonies always performed in the same manner

sacred relating to religious beliefs or practices

soldering process of joining different pieces of metal by heating them

solstice period when the sun is farthest away from the earth's equator – this occurs twice a year, once in the summer and once in the winter

tattoo permanent pattern made by inserting a dye underneath human skin

teepee portable living structure used by the Plains Indians and made from buffalo skins

totem poles carved and painted cedar logs that tell the history of clans and their religious beliefs

trait distinguishing feature

unprecedented having never before happened

vision quest act of seeking spiritual messages or guidance through isolated prayer and contemplation

Index

Titles in the *World Art and Culture* series include:

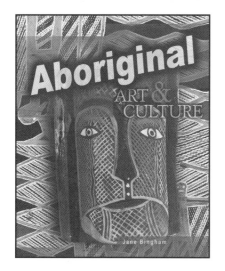

Hardback 1 844 21054 5

Hardback 1 844 21044 8

Hardback 1 844 21055 3

Hardback 1 844 21046 4

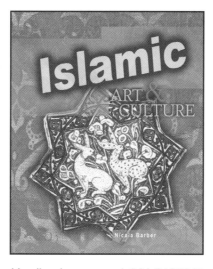

Hardback 1 844 21053 7

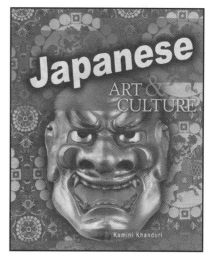

Hardback 1 844 21043 X

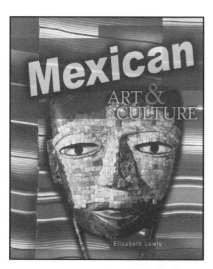

Hardback 1 844 21045 6

Hardback 1 844 21056 1

Find out about other Raintree titles on our website www.raintreepublishers.co.uk